PLUTO'S SECRET

An Icy World's Tale of Discovery

By Margaret A. Weitekamp
with David DeVorkin

Illustrated by Diane Kidd

Published in association with the
Smithsonian National Air and Space Museum

Abrams Books for Young Readers, New York

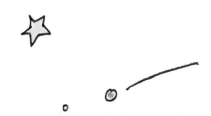

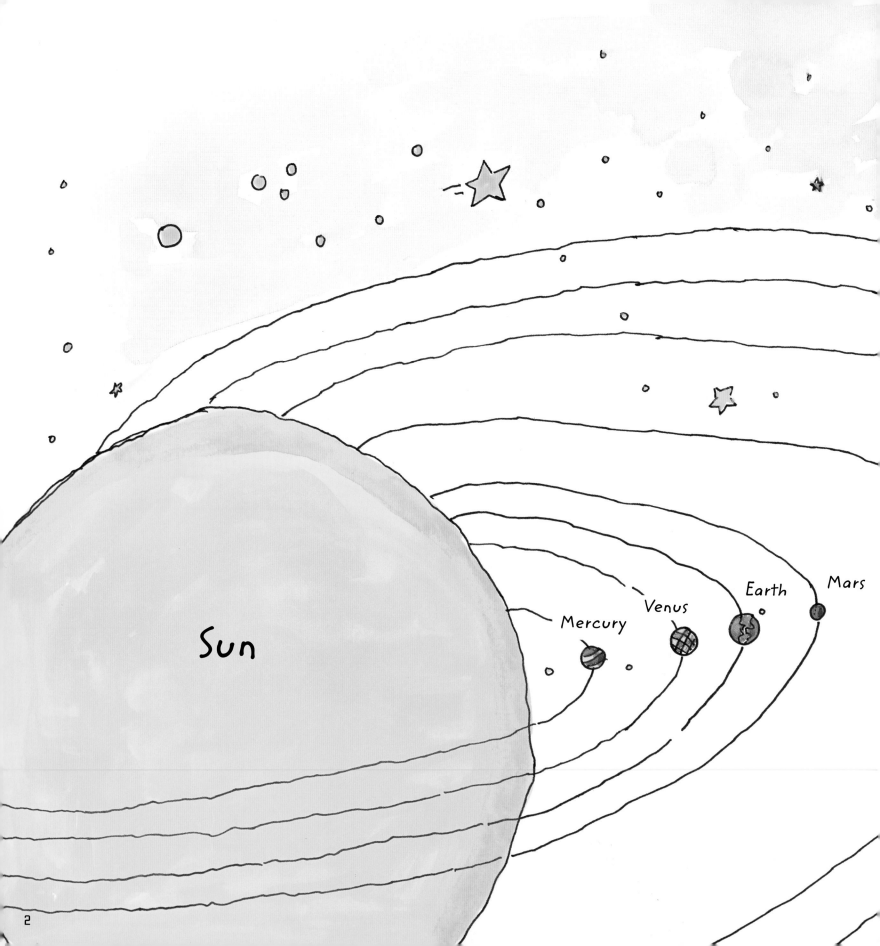

Sun

Mercury

Venus

Earth

Mars

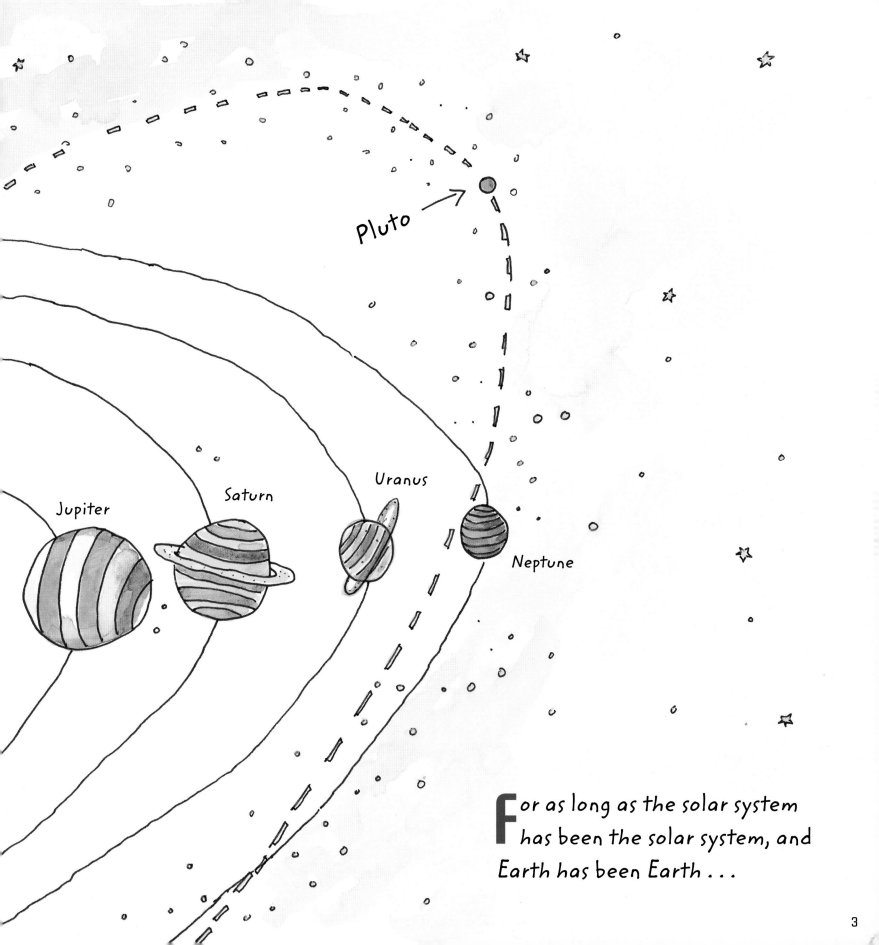

Pluto

Jupiter

Saturn

Uranus

Neptune

For as long as the solar system has been the solar system, and Earth has been Earth . . .

. . . there has been a little icy world circling the sun, farther away than any of the planets.

This icy world had a secret—a clue about something that exists in the solar system and the universe.

But for a long time, no one on Earth could see this icy world. It was too far away and not bright enough to be seen in the sky. And so no one learned its secret.

The icy world didn't mind.
It was busy dancing with its
moons.

Cha-cha
Cha-cha-cha

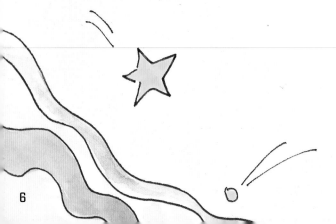

a = The semi-major axis of the inner planet.

ℓ = its mean longitude.

e = its eccentricity.

ϖ = The longitude of its perihelion.

a', ℓ', e', ϖ', are the corresponding values for the outer planet.

mutual inclination of the orbits. $\ell_0 = \ell - \ell'$

$$a = \frac{a}{a'}$$

STAR CHART

In the early 1900s, Percival Lowell, a very wealthy man from Boston, decided to look for a ninth planet. He knew that eight planets went around the sun. They were Mercury, Venus, Mars, Jupiter, Saturn, Uranus, and Neptune—and, of course, Earth (the planet that Percival was standing on!).

Along with other astronomers (people who study the universe and how it works), Percival believed that something was pulling on the paths (or the "orbits") of Uranus and Neptune. He had already built the Lowell Observatory in Arizona to study Mars. Now he ordered his staff of astronomers to search for a new planet beyond Neptune.

"What is out there?" he asked.

"There must be another planet, a GREAT BIG ONE—a bully that's causing all this trouble, that's bothering Uranus and Neptune" was Percival's answer to himself. "I shall call this mysterious planet

Planet X."

"Planet X! A great big one?" thought the little icy world. "That's not right. Wait until they see how lightly I dance with my moon Charon, the tiny tots Nix and Hydra, and the other little ones! Besides, I'm not bothering anyone!"

The icy world kept doing what it liked to do: spin on its side.

ZOOM, ZOOM, ZOOM!

Percival's astronomers looked and looked for Planet X. After Percival died in 1916, they looked even harder. They wanted to prove that Percival had been right.

In the late 1920s, the Lowell Observatory hired a young fellow named Clyde Tombaugh (pronounced TOM-bah) to keep on searching. With a powerful new telescopic camera, Clyde took pictures of the night sky where he was told the new planet might be. Finally, in 1930, he found something!

In one of the pictures, Clyde saw a very small dot among thousands of other dots of many sizes, the stars. A few days later, another picture of the same area showed the same dot—but this time it was in a different place! Clyde knew that planets do that: they appear to move among the stars. (The word planet comes from the Greek word for "wanderer.")

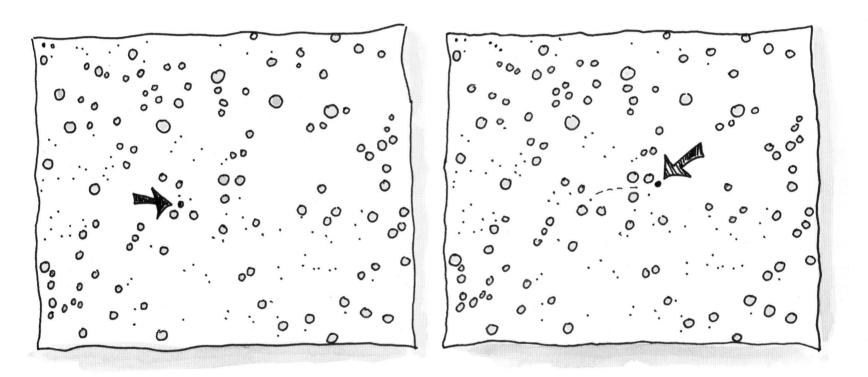

"Hello, Earth!" said the icy world. But Clyde couldn't hear as he was very, very far away.

"I have found Planet X!" Clyde said.

MINERVA?

CRONUS?

"There is a ninth planet in our solar system!" declared Lowell's astronomers on March 13, 1930. They wanted to tell everyone the exciting news on what would have been Percival Lowell's birthday.

People from all over the world suggested names for the new planet.

"What about Minerva?"

LOWELL?

"No," said the astronomers.

"Certainly not!" thought the icy little world.

ATLAS?

"How about Cronus?"

"Nope," said the astronomers.

"Yikes!" said the icy world. "That's not me."

"Zeus? Atlas? Lowell?"

"No, no, no," said the astronomers.

"Yuck!" thought the little world.

YUCK!

Then eleven-year-old Venetia Burney from Oxford, England, suggested the name *Pluto*.

"Because," said Venetia, whose class had studied the Greek and Roman gods as well as the solar system, "Pluto is the Roman god of the dark underworld. The new little planet is so far from the sun that it must be a cold, dark place too."

"I like that!" thought the icy world, which was now named Pluto.

Pluto, Roman god of the dark underworld

Venetia Burney, 11-year-old girl

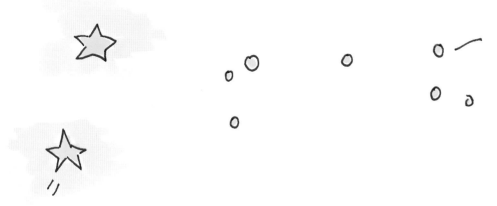

"But . . . a planet?" Pluto thought. "Just like the other planets? That's not correct. None of the other planets are as little as I am. And the other planets have very ordinary flat orbits around the sun, like a tabletop. My orbit is much more fun! It tips up like a slide in the playground."

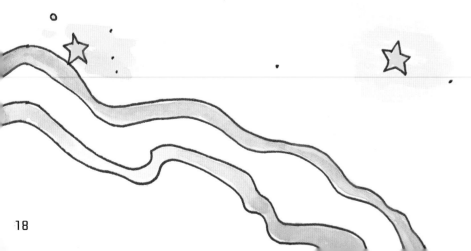

"Whee!"

The astronomers soon learned that Pluto did not always stay in its place. Sometimes it even switched places with Neptune, coming closer to the sun than Neptune did.

"Hey!" yelled the astronomers. "Planets cannot do that!"

"Well, I can and I do!" Pluto giggled.

Remember, the icy world Pluto had a secret—a clue about what exists at the outer edges of the solar system and across the universe.

"You still have not figured me out!" sang Pluto. "Keep trying!"

Many years after Clyde Tombaugh first found Pluto, when astronomers were looking at the icy world with newer, more powerful telescopes, they saw that it was not alone.

Pluto had friends in orbits very much like its own. This meant that there were other icy worlds. Some of Pluto's friends were just about as big as it was.

"Say 'cheese'!" Pluto told its friends, as the various high-powered telescopes took their picture.

Astronomers named the area where these new objects orbited "the Kuiper belt," after the astronomer who first predicted it, Gerard Kuiper (rhymes with "piper"). The Kuiper belt was a whole new part of the solar system.

"Now you're getting closer." Pluto smiled. "You're on the right track!"

"Oh Pluto!" The astronomers sighed. "You're not like the other planets. We sometimes wonder if you should even be called a planet."

And then they thought, "Hmm . . . what exactly is a planet?"

Amazingly, no one had ever set up rules about what a planet was—or was not.

In 2006, because of Pluto, the astronomers voted on a definition.

"Planets have to orbit the sun," the astronomers decided.

"I go around the sun in an orbit," thought Pluto.

"Planets have to be round, like a ball," said the astronomers.

"I'm round," Pluto thought.

"Each planet has to be alone in its orbit."

"But my friends are with me! We all go around the sun in the Kuiper belt."

"Then Pluto is not a planet!"

the astronomers declared.

Some people were sad that Pluto was not called a planet anymore. But Pluto didn't mind. It liked orbiting with its friends.

"You figured it out!" Pluto reassured them. "I'm not a planet. I'm the first example of something new. I'm one of many icy worlds on the edge of the solar system."

Pluto thought that it was fun that so many people were wondering about what to call it now. Perhaps "dwarf planet"? Or maybe "Kuiper belt object"?

"I'm not worried. Whatever you call me, I'm fine out here," said Pluto.

NEW HORIZONS
SPACECRAFT

30

But Pluto held clues to more than just our solar system. As astronomers looked for planets around other stars, they saw bands of icy worlds around other stars too.

"Ah, my secret is out!" said Pluto. "Not only do I have friends here, but there are also bands of icy worlds just like me around other stars all over the universe."

Pluto had helped astronomers to define what a planet is—and also to recognize the icy worlds around other stars. In 2015, the New Horizons spacecraft will be Pluto's first visitor from Earth.

"I can't wait!" says Pluto. "I may even have some other secrets to reveal. Get ready!"

 *Cha-cha-cha!*

The People and Telescopes Behind the Story

LEFT: Percival Lowell peers through his large telescope at his observatory in Flagstaff, Arizona. Lowell wished to observe the planet Mars.

BELOW, LEFT: After Lowell died, Clyde Tombaugh was hired to look beyond Mars and seek photographs of Planet X, the planet that Lowell believed existed beyond the known planets.

BELOW: Lowell's telescopic camera. It allows the viewer to take photographs of objects far away, such as planets, icy worlds, and stars. The photographic plate was placed at the bottom of the thick tube. Clyde guided the exposure through the thin-tubed telescope.

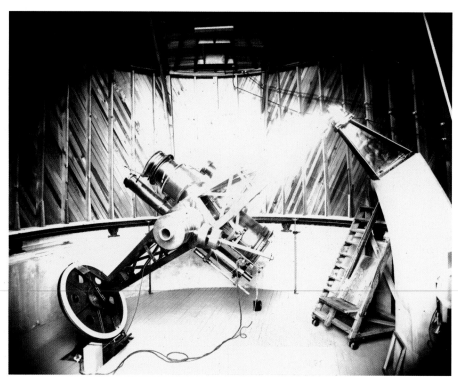

RIGHT: This is the telescopic camera that Clyde Tombaugh used to photograph Pluto. A 13-inch lens sits on the top of the large tube and focuses a wide field of stars onto the photographic plate (the plate sits inside the gray plateholder at the bottom of the tube). The plate is exposed for many minutes—up to a few hours—using the thin tube beneath the telescopic camera as a guide. Clyde would sit for hours making sure the big camera followed the stars perfectly. If this camera was in operation it would be looking through an opening in the dome. When the telescopic camera is not in use, the opening is closed.

BELOW: The real Pluto discovery plates! These two plates, or photographs, show the same star field. They have been exposed at different times and show a spot of light has moved between the first and second exposures. This movement is what a planet would do, and is how Clyde discovered Pluto (which is the spot of light to which the arrow is pointing!).

BELOW, RIGHT: Eleven-year-old Venetia Burney of Oxford, England, who named Pluto.

January 23, 1930

January 29, 1930

Who's Who

VENETIA BURNEY: The girl who suggested the name Pluto. Grandniece of Henry Madan, the man who named Mars's moons, Phobos and Deimos.

EARTH: Our home, the largest of the rocky planets in our solar system, and the third from the sun. A fine little planet with oceans, large land bodies, and ice caps.

JUPITER: The largest known planet in our solar system, the fifth from the sun. A planet made principally of gas, liquid, and ice, with a solid core. A giant storm (the Great Red Spot) has raged in its atmosphere for centuries. Several Earth probes have flown past Jupiter, and the spacecraft *Galileo* orbited the planet for seven years beginning in 1995.

KUIPER BELT: A region of the solar system far beyond the orbit of Neptune, where countless thousands of icy bodies like Pluto orbit the sun.

PERCIVAL LOWELL: Member of a very rich Boston family who devoted his life to travel and writing on many subjects. He built an observatory in Flagstaff, Arizona, to study Mars.

MARS: A small rocky planet traveling in an orbit fourth from the sun. Called the "red planet" because it appears red when viewed with a telescope. Many spacecraft have explored Mars, either from orbit or on its surface. Recently, mobile landers called "rovers," including Pathfinder's *Sojourner* in 1997 and the Mars Exploration rovers *Spirit* and *Opportunity*, which landed in 2004, have traveled across the Martian surface. The Mars Science Laboratory *Curiosity* landed in 2012.

MERCURY: A rocky planet and the closest known planet to the sun. The *MESSENGER* (MErcury Surface, Space ENvironment, GEochemistry, and Ranging) spacecraft that began orbiting it in 2011 is only the second spacecraft ever to visit Mercury.

NEPTUNE: The first major planet discovered not by sighting it in the sky but by mathematical prediction. Much larger than Earth, it is still the smallest of the gas giant planets like Jupiter. It is the eighth planet from the sun. In 1988, *Voyager 2* provided the first color pictures of Neptune. (*Voyager 2* is now more than 14 billion kilometers from Earth—and still going!)

PLUTO: A small round icy world that made astronomers rethink what a planet is. About as big around as Alaska is wide, Pluto was discovered after an intense search for planets beyond Neptune that might have been disturbing the orbits of Neptune and Uranus.

SATURN: A gas giant planet second only to Jupiter in size and sixth from the sun. Saturn has a spectacular system of rings made of millions of small rocky and icy bodies. The Cassini-Huygens mission that reached Saturn in 2004 involved seventeen different countries, organized by NASA, the European Space Agency, and the Italian Space Agency.

SUN: Our central star that gives the Earth and planets light and heat. It's a great glowing globe of gas, mainly hydrogen and helium.

CLYDE TOMBAUGH: The self-taught telescope builder and astronomer who was living on his parents' Kansas farm when he was hired at the age of twenty-three by the Lowell Observatory to search for Planet X—and found it!

URANUS (pronounced YUR-an-us): The first planet discovered since long, long ago, and the first discovered using a telescope (by William Herschel, who initially thought that he'd seen a comet). The seventh in order from the sun. In 1986, *Voyager 2* became the only spacecraft to visit Uranus when it passed the planet on its way to Neptune and beyond.

VENUS: Earth's twin, slightly smaller, in an orbit smaller than Earth's and the second planet from the sun. Known as both "the morning star" and "the evening star." It is constantly shrouded in dense clouds of sulfuric acid and carbon dioxide. (Pee-yew!) In 1966, the Soviet *Venera 3* probe became the first human-made object to strike another planet's surface when it crash-landed on Venus.

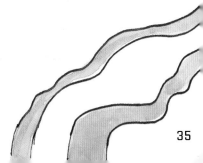

Glossary

ASTRONOMER: A person who asks questions about how the universe and all the things in it came to be, how they are organized, and what will happen to them in the future.

GAS PLANETS: Planets made of gas with surface features that change.

GRAVITY: The pull that every object creates, a force of attraction caused by the presence of matter.

MOON: A world orbiting another world that is not a star.

OBSERVATORY: A building where telescopes are housed and are used to explore the universe.

ORBIT: The path of a planet around a star, or the path of any object around another object. A planet's orbit is shaped like a squashed circle called an ellipse (pronounced "ee-LIPS" *).

PLANET: A ball-shaped object that circles a star, is alone in its orbit, and shines only by the reflected light from that star.

ROCKY PLANETS: Planets made up of solid substances that have solid surfaces with consistent features.

SOLAR SYSTEM: The collection of planets, comets, meteors, gas, dust, and worlds of many types that circle a star such as our sun.

STARS: Great globes of glowing gases that shine with their own light. Our sun is an average star. There are stars as big as the orbit of Saturn and stars smaller in size than Earth.

TELESCOPE: A device that makes distant objects appear close by and brighter.

TELESCOPIC CAMERA: A telescope with a built-in camera.

UNIVERSE: Everything that exists.

WORLD: Any object in space.

* EASY EXPERIMENT: What's an ellipse? Tonight at dinner, take your round dinner plate, hold it up, and look at it straight on. That's a circle. Now, tilt your plate a teeny bit. The shape you see now is what a planet's orbital path looks like! Scientists call this shape an "ellipse." It's a special kind of oval. (Be sure to clean up the mess that you made on the table.)

A Note from the Museum

In 2006, the scientists of the International Astronomical Union (IAU), the worldwide organization that decides the names and rules of astronomy, gathered in Prague, Czech Republic, for their regular meeting. The astronomers faced a historic decision. Discoveries of icy worlds in the region of space occupied by Pluto had raised questions. If Pluto was a planet, were these other bodies also planets? And, if they were not, how could Pluto continue to be one?

For the first time, astronomers voted on the exact definition of a planet. (People had always assumed that they knew what a planet was, much as people know what a continent is. But there was no official definition.) As a result, Pluto was removed from the list of planets that so many schoolchildren had memorized for decades. Instead, the IAU declared that Pluto was a "dwarf planet."

We are living in a golden age of astronomy. Using new instruments, astronomers are making new discoveries and improving what we know on a daily basis. All that change is a part of science, the search for new knowledge. Scientists will continue to uncover the secrets of Pluto—and the rest of the universe—for years to come.

Acknowledgments

Thank you to Howard W. Reeves, James B. Armstrong, Zachary Brown, Chad Beckerman, Robyn Ng, and Alison Gervais at Abrams for all of their hard work to make this book happen. Special thanks to Trish Graboske at the Smithsonian Air and Space Museum for shepherding this project from start to finish. Thank you also to the Conrad N. Hilton Foundation for its support of early childhood education at the Museum.

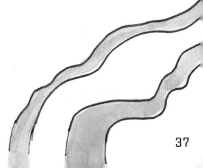

Suggested Reading for Young People

Children of the Sun by Arthur John L'Hommedieu, Child's Play (International) Ltd, 1993

Comets, Stars, the Moon, and Mars: Space Poems and Paintings by Douglas Florian, Harcourt, Inc, 2007

Dogs in Space by Nancy Coffelt, Voyager Books, Harcourt, Brace & Company, 1993

Faces of the Moon by Bob Crelin, illustrated by Leslie Evans, Charlesbridge Publishing, 2009

Find the Constellations by H. A. Rey, revised edition, HMH Books, 1976

Meet the Planets by John McGranaghan and Laurie Allen Klein, Sylvan Dell Publishing, 2011

Our Solar System by Seymour Simon, revised edition, Collins, 2007

Saturn for My Birthday by John McGranaghan, Sylvan Dell Publishing, 2008

There Once Was A Sky Full of Stars by Bob Crelin, Sky Publishing Corp., 2003

There's No Place Like Space: All About Our Solar System by Tish Rabe and Aristides Ruiz, revised edition, Cat in the Hat's Learning Library, Random House Books for Young Readers, 1999

There's Nothing to Do on Mars by Chris Gall, Little Brown, 2008

Bibliography

BOOKS

Brown, Mike. *How I Killed Pluto and Why It Had It Coming* (New York: Spiegel & Grau, 2010).

Tyson, Neil deGrasse. *The Pluto Files: The Rise and Fall of America's Favorite Planet* (New York: W.W. Norton & Company, 2009).

JOURNALS

Sky and Telescope
http://www.skyandtelescope.com

Astronomy
http://www.astronomy.com/News-Observing/Astronomy%20Kids.aspx

WEBSITES

International Astronomical Union's Web page on Pluto: http://www.iau.org/public/pluto/

Lowell Observatory's Web site: http://www.lowell.edu

NASA's New Horizons Web site: http://www.nasa.gov/mission_pages/newhorizons/main/index.html

Smithsonian National Air and Space Museum's "Exploring the Planets" Web site: http://airandspace.si.edu/research/ceps/etp/pluto

Index

The art for this book was created using Windsor Newton water-colors, pen and ink, and colored pencils on Arches watercolor paper.

The Library of Congress has already cataloged a prior printing under LCCN: 2012033546

ISBN for hardcover edition: 978-1-4197-0423-9
ISBN for this edition: 978-1-4197-1526-6

Text and illustrations copyright © 2013 National Air and Space Museum, Smithsonian Institution

Photograph of Venetia Burney is courtesy of Patrick Phair.
All other photographs courtesy of Lowell Observatory Archives.

Book design by Robyn Ng

Printed and bound in China
10 9 8 7 6 5 4 3 2 1

Abrams Books for Young Readers are available at special discounts when purchased in quantity for premiums and promotions as well as fundraising or educational use. Special editions can also be created to specification. For details, contact specialsales@abramsbooks.com or the address below.

ABRAMS
THE ART OF BOOKS SINCE 1949

115 West 18th Street
New York, NY 10011
www.abramsbooks.com

For Xavier, whose love of stories inspired this book, and Kati and Quincy, who light up my world. —M.W.

To Percival, Clyde, and Zenobia. —D.D.

For my family, friends, NASM ED staff, Exhibits, Howard R., Ga-Ga, and intern Richard B. for all your support and for sharing my orbit. —D.K.